CW00501032

How to play golf quickly!

By John Timpson

First published in 2005. Written by John Timpson CBE.

Copyright © John Timpson 2005.

ISBN 0-9547049-4-0

Timpson House, Claverton Road, Wythenshawe, Manchester M23 9TT.

Sensible speed

Before signing up to the Society of
Quick Golfers it's worth asking why
it is a good thing to spend less time
on the golf course.

Pure pleasure

It's more fun getting on with the
game and spending less time
between shots.

More energy

Quick golf is a lot less tiring – it's the time you spend on your feet that makes you weary and after 3 hours fatigue sets in.

Creates more time

You can put time saved on the golf
course to positive advantage.

Quick golfers get more out of life.

Success rate

During a quick round you keep your
concentration and your swing – there
is no doubt about it, the faster you
play the better you score.

No speed limit

Play slow golf if you want but…

Let faster
players through!

Fast habits

Quick golfers do a few simple
things that save a lot of
time over 18 holes.

CARRY YOUR CLUBS

No trollies

If you carry your clubs you walk in
a straight line – straight along
the green and right through
areas where trolleys are forbidden.

Save ⅓ mile a round!

CARRY LESS CLUBS

Club selection

The scores in a five club competition
are as good as those returned
with a full set of 14.

Avoid big bags

Some bags are so big you need a caddie and a trolley to help him carry them.

Leave big bags to the professionals.

CHECK EXCESS BAGGAGE

Travel light

Only carry things you need…

On hot sunny days leave your
umbrella and waterproofs behind.

WALK QUICKLY

Healthy exercise

It does you good to
increase the heart rate.

BE PREPARED

Be ready to play

Keep things moving by being
prepared to take your turn.

PLAY OUT OF TURN

Abandon stragglers

Don't wait for a wayward member
of your party. As soon as you
are ready… play on.

THINK AHEAD

Prepare to tee off

Arrive on the next tee with ball
and tee peg in hand.

FOLLOW YOUR BALL

Super spotter

Take very careful note of where
your ball goes – good ball
spotting saves a lot of time.

RELOAD

Play a provisional

When playing in a medal if in doubt
reload – it could be the biggest
timesaver of your round.

HOLD THE FLAG

Standard bearer

If you've putted out, take charge of the
flag. It's good form, saves time and
takes your mind off the worry of
the next drive.

HELP STRANGERS

Generous host

If you're playing with a visitor, be kind and show them the right line for blind shots – it saves time spent looking for lost balls.

Misleading directions could provoke the same tactic when you play on their course.

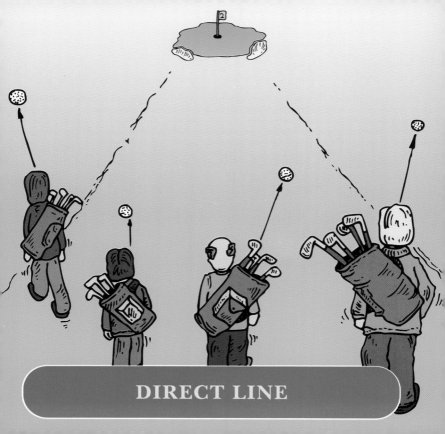

DIRECT LINE

Walk straight to your ball

Never mind about anyone
else – take a direct line towards
your own ball – it is the quickest
route round the course.

READY TO GO

Bag positioning

Leave your bag on the right side
of the green – on the way
to your next destination.

PLAN YOUR PUTT

Be prepared

Work out the line of your putt while

you are waiting for your turn –

it cuts putting time in half!

Give putts

Holeing out putts takes a lot of time – it's often a good idea to give some missable putts and claim the moral high ground.

FORGO YOUR FOURBALL

Play foursomes

If you want a really quick game play
foursomes – it's the best test
of golf and a lot of fun.

TIME WASTERS

So slow

Some people simply don't get on
with the game – here are some
of the things that hold them up.

CHATTERBOXES

Stop talking

If you want a chat get round
quickly so you have plenty of
time to talk in the bar.

Fore play

How long does everyone have to
wait for you to hit the ball?

**Two practice swings are
enough for anybody.**

WALKING TOGETHER

Formation fourball

There is no need to walk in formation.

If you hit the ball in different directions
walk apart and meet at the green.

LOOKING FOR
A LOST CAUSE

Give up

There is no point in wasting time looking
in the wilderness – even if you find
your ball it will be unplayable.

THREE OFF THE TEE

Going back to play another

Playing 3 off the tee is only worthwhile
if you are well placed in a medal – even
then you probably should have
played a provisional.

Far too social

Some people walk across two fairways simply to say hello. Save time by concentrating on your own game and keep your conversation for the clubhouse.

CHANGE OF CLOTHING

Cover up

Cautious golfers change into waterproofs
at the slightest sign of wet weather.
But waterproofs waste a lot of time.

If it rains put up your umbrella and
if it becomes a deluge, walk back
to the club house.

Off the leash

Most dog owners are fast golfers –
they like to walk quickly.

But badly behaved dogs cause
havoc – leave them at home.

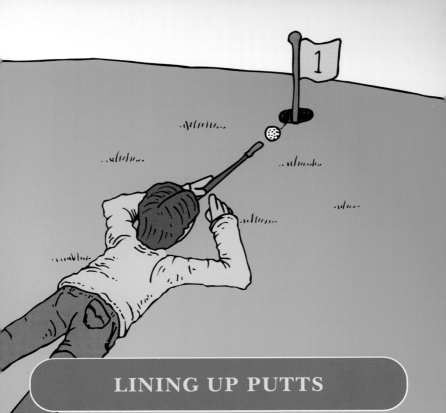

LINING UP PUTTS

Town hall clocks

Some people look as if they are
playing in the Open Championship.
Studying the line from every angle
takes a lot of time when you take
42 putts a round.

PUTTING OUT FOR A 7

Holeing out

Some golfers insist on putting when
the hole is well and truly lost.

Save the putt for the next
hole – when it might matter.

Green additions

Good golfers know the score.
Clear the green before you
fill in your card

NEXT TEE

POOR PARKING

Thoughtlessness

Think ahead.

Always leave your clubs

en-route to the next tee.

RAKEMANSHIP

Sense in the sand

Before playing a bunker shot collect the rake and place it nearby - that way you won't spend so long in the bunker.

Overtaking

Experienced golfers know when to let the people behind go through. Here are some simple guidelines.

LOST BALL

Lost ball

If, when looking for a ball,
people are waiting, call
them through immediately.

LOST TOUCH

Clear hole ahead

If you lose touch with the game
in front and people are waiting
behind let them through.

KNOWN SPEED MERCHANTS

Fast lane

If someone is clearly quicker
than you, make life easy let them
through as soon as you can.

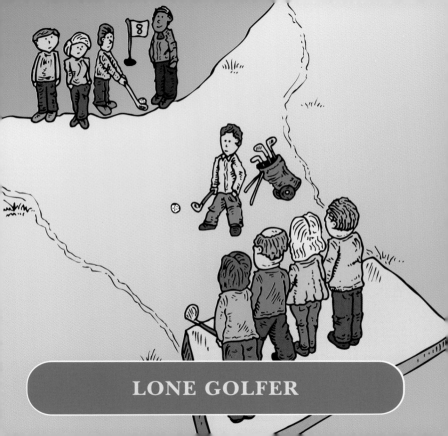

LONE GOLFER

Crowded out

Lone golfers have no standing – if you
are squeezed between two groups walk
off and find a quiet part of the course.

Chivalry

There is no shame in letting people through – it's good etiquette and should be done with style.

The secret

Seize the moral high ground
by inviting people through
before they expect it.

Held up hints

Being held up can cause
golfers to act badly.

**Don't be tempted
to lose your temper.**

KEEP COOL

Be patient

Give the people in front one hole
to do the decent thing.

Hands on hips

Drop clubs

BANG

Frantic practice swings

Lie down

DESPERATE MEASURES

Gentle hints

These tactics are not good etiquette
but what can you do if you are
held up – anyway they often work.

Gross negligence

However frustrating the situation

NEVER

hit out when they are in range.

Ask politely

If you have to ask the question use your most charming voice and make the request more in sorrow than anger.

Tact

Frank talking can be misinterpreted.
Never suggest someone else is too
slow – just apologise for being quick.

Never chastise

REMEMBER – The person you criticize on the course will meet you again in the clubhouse.

Thank with style

Show your gratitude – they might be holding you up again next week.

RECOGNISE ANYBODY?

Mrs Quick

Talkative Tina

Carol Cardmarker

Society Simon

Harry Hacker

Peter Poser

Sid Saunter

Stubborn Stanley

Terry Tortoise

Fidgeting Frank

Master Champion

Character spotting

You can spot people's attitude to golf as they walk to the first tee – do you know any of these characters.

Mrs Quick

A woman on a mission, she hardly
stops walking to play a shot –
don't get in her way.

Harry Hacker

Harry claims to enjoy golf enormously —
but only plays twice a year.

Says sorry 100 times a round and often
competes in corporate golf days.

Stubborn Stanley

Stan is a bit of a snob – he has been golfing since childhood and knows all you need to know about the game.

He last let someone through in 1976 and is growing more cussed with age. He is unlikely to let anyone through again.

Talkative Tina

On a clear day you can hear every detail
of Tina's conversation 250 yards away.

It's no wonder she can't remember
how many shots it has taken
to get on the green.

Peter Poser

Peter has every golf gadget going but his wife still gives him more every Christmas.

But he hasn't got is a copy of this book – he graces the golf course for at least 4 hours every round.

Terry Tortoise

Terry has an electric trolley with only one speed – at a distance he moves like a ship on the horizon. Fortunately Terry often only plays 9 holes.

Carol Cardmarker

Carol has yet to catch the magic of match play – she plays all her games against the course. She isn't a quitter – every hole is played to the final putt.

Sid Saunter

Sid enjoys the golf course – he appreciates the gorse and the Canada Geese. It's great to be out in the fresh air and being close to nature. Occasionally he hits the ball.

Fidgeting Frank

Fidgeting Frank drives playing partners round
the bend. On your back swing, Frank
suddenly gets out a tissue to blow his
nose. Frank spoils your swing, slows
your play and increases your score,
but is, totally unaware of your distress.

WHY PLAY QUICKLY?

Society Simon

If you arrive for a quick weekday nine holes
and the car park is full of solicitors, go home
and wash the dog. Society Simon is the one
with the baseball cap, he is in no mood for
quick golf. Having looked forward to the
outing for weeks. He is going to make a
day of it – dinner isn't until 7.15.

Master Champion

This young golfer is already down to single figures and takes the game very seriously. He plays slightly slower than Bernhard Langer.

HOW DO YOU RATE ☞

Mr Quick   *Mrs Average*   *Mr Slow*

Fill in your best time

FORMAT	TIME *Hrs/Mins*	WHO DID YOU PLAY WITH
Foursome		
2 Ball		
3 Ball		
4 Ball		

Check your rating!

(In hours and minutes)

Format	Quick	Good	Average	Slow	V.Slow	Painful
Foursome	2.30	2.45	3.00	3.20	3.40	4.00
2 Ball	2.40	3.00	3.15	3.30	3.50	4.10
3 Ball	2.50	3.10	3.30	3.45	4.00	4.15
4 Ball	3.00	3.20	3.40	4.00	4.15	4.40